COCKTAILS

DEVELOPED BY

WILLIAMS SONOMA

TEST KITCHEN

Photographs John Kernick

weldon**owen**

COCKTAIL HOUR

There is something so satisfying about shaking up a frosty combination of spirits, ice, and mixers and creating a magical concoction. Whether you're sipping a refreshing mix of gin and citrus on a summer night or warming up with a cozy combination of bourbon and vanilla at a holiday gathering, cocktails turn any occasion into a festive one.

This indispensable guide contains all the tips and tools needed to master the art of creating cocktails at home, from choosing the right glass to mastering party-ready ice cubes. Learn the formula for crafting the perfect cocktail with more than 40 new recipes that marry modernity with tradition. Enjoy a Lime & Thyme Gin Fizz (page 34) to unwind after a long day or make a big bowl of Cranberry-Tequila Punch (page 58) for your next fête. And no cocktail hour would be complete without tempting bar snacks—Brown Butter & Rosemary Popcorn (page 82), Tamari-Maple Mixed Nuts (page 88), and Crispy Curried Chickpeas (page 91) bring delicious flavors and crunch to any drinks gathering.

Today's inspired flavor combinations bring a contemporary profile to our favorite cocktails that is contributing to a new and intensely flavorful era of mixed drinks. Our collection of timeless recipes, paired with our guide to essential bar tools and glassware, top-notch ingredients, and garnish options, will get you on your way to mastering mixology. With this inspiring handbook on the bar, you'll be mixing up the perfect cocktail for every season, occasion, and mood. Cheers!

Cocktail Picks

Ice Pick

Ice Bucket & Tongs

Channel Knife

Bar Spoons

TOOLS OF THE TRADE

Having a good selection of tools on hand will up your cocktail game and spruce up your home bar. Find a complete guide to the essentials on page 8.

Julep Strainer

Measuring Cup

Stainless Steel Cocktail Shaker

Mixing Glass

Glass Cocktail Shaker

Jigger

Cocktail Napkins

Hawthorne Strainer

Dripless Bottle Pourer

Corkscrew Wine Opener

Measuring Spoons

ESSENTIAL BAR TOOLS

When creating a cocktail, begin with high-quality ingredients and a well-stocked bar. Beyond those basics, these indispensable tools will set you up with everything you need to bartend with ease and success.

JUICERS

Essential for preparing drinks with fresh citrus, juicers come in many shapes and sizes. A hand-held citrus squeezer is great for lemons and limes, while a citrus reamer is ideal for bigger citrus fruits like grapefruits and oranges. Juicers work well for both fruits and vegetables.

JIGGER

This small liquid measurement tool comes in both an hourglass shape (page 7) and a small measuring cup style—the former best for speed, the latter for precision.

MUDDLER

Use this baseball bat–shaped tool for crushing fruits, herbs, and sugar cubes. Look for ones made of solid wood with a flat head and long enough to clear the edge of the glass.

BAR SPOON

This long-handled spoon is also known as a cocktail or mixing spoon. It is used to stir drinks in a pitcher or shaker, or for crushing sugar, fruits, or herb leaves.

CHANNEL KNIFE

The v-shaped blade on this stout bar knife cuts long thin strips of citrus for use as a garnish.

SHAKER

No bar would be complete without this iconic tool that provides the double function of mixing and chilling. A cocktail shaker quickly and effectively cools down and mixes cocktail ingredients, but also develops texture in the finished drink.

Boston Shaker A two-part shaker consisting of a pint glass or metal cup and metal canister. Place ingredients in the pint glass or cup, secure the metal canister firmly on top to create a seal, then turn and shake. Strain the drink from the metal canister into a glass.

Cobbler Shaker A three-part shaker with a built-in strainer and snug-fitting top.

STRAINER

This useful addition to your home bar keeps ice and other solid ingredients inside a shaker when you're pouring the cocktail into a glass.

Hawthorne Strainer The coiled springs around the rim of this basic cocktail strainer ensure a snug fit with most canisters and glasses, making it a good choice for either shaken or stirred drinks.

Julep Strainer The round, perforated bowl of this cocktail strainer looks like an oversized slotted spoon and works well for stirred drinks.

GUIDE TO GLASSWARE

The shape of the glass affects both the flavor and aroma of a drink, not to mention the final presentation. Use the guide below to make the best selection for every cocktail. To help keep iced drinks cold, chill glasses before pouring.

MARTINI GLASS

Use this James Bond–worthy glass for any drink served "up" (chilled, then strained).

Cocktail pairing: Pomegranate Martini (page 23)

ROCKS GLASS

Also known as an old-fashioned glass, this short and stocky tumbler is used primarily for drinks served on the rocks (over ice).

Cocktail pairing: Grapefruit & Sage Gimlet (page 33)

HIGHBALL

This tall glass keeps bubbles intact, so it's perfect for drinks with carbonation served over ice.

Cocktail pairing: Strawberry-Lillet Vodka Soda (page 16)

COLLINS GLASS

Taller and narrower than a highball glass, this is named for the Tom Collins cocktail and is ideal when a tall and frosty glass is desired.

Cocktail pairing: Elderflower-Rose Collins (page 35)

COUPE GLASS

The shallow, broad bowl of this design is ideal for shaken or stirred cocktails that are strained into a glass with no ice.

Cocktail pairing: Tarragon Negroni (page 36)

CHAMPAGNE FLUTE

The tall, slender bowl of this romantic glass showcases and preserves the effervescence of any sparkling drink.

Cocktail pairing: French 75 with Lavender & Lemon (page 30)

JULEP CUP

Although this gleaming silver cup is designed for mint juleps, it works well with any drink that has crushed ice, as the metal material helps to keep the drink cold.

Cocktail pairing: Basil Julep (page 52)

COPPER MUG

This elegant mug is typically used for Moscow mules, but is well suited for any drink with ice and soda.

Cocktail pairing: Meyer Lemon–Rosemary Moscow Mule (page 24)

PUNCH BOWL

This big glass or other nonreactive bowl is great for entertaining and big parties.

Cocktail pairing: Cranberry-Tequila Punch (page 58)

Punch Bowl

Coupe Glass

Martini Glass

Collins Glass

Julep Cup

RAISE A GLASS

Choosing the right glass is key for both presentation and taste. Dress up your cocktail with the appropriate selection from this handsome array of sparkling barware.

Stemless Wine Glass

Highball

Champagne
Flute

White Wine
Glass

Glass Pitcher

Rocks Glass

Tumbler

Rocks Glass

Copper
Mug

THE CLASSICS

SHAKEN

COSMOPOLITAN

2 oz (60 ml) vodka
¾ oz (45 ml) lime juice
¼ oz (15 ml) cranberry juice
½ oz (30 ml) triple sec
1 lime slice

In a cocktail shaker filled with ice, combine the vodka, lime juice, cranberry juice, and triple sec. Cover and shake vigorously. Strain into a chilled coupe glass. Garnish with the lime slice.

TOM COLLINS

2 oz (60 ml) gin
½ oz (15 ml) fresh lemon juice
½ oz (15 ml) simple syrup
5-6 oz (150-180 ml) club soda
1 lemon wedge

In a cocktail shaker filled with ice, combine the gin, lemon juice, and simple syrup. Cover and shake vigorously. Strain into an ice-filled Collins glass. Top with the club soda and stir. Garnish with the lemon wedge.

WHISKEY SOUR

2 oz (60 ml) blended Canadian Whiskey
¾ oz (22 ml) fresh lemon juice
½ oz (15 ml) simple syrup (page 92)
1 orange slice
1 maraschino cherry

Fill a cocktail shaker with ice. Add the whisky, lemon juice, and simple syrup and shake vigorously. Strain into chilled rocks or couple glass. Garnish with the orange slice and maraschino cherry.

DRY MARTINI

3 oz (90 ml) gin
½ oz (15 ml) dry vermouth
1 martini olive

In a cocktail shaker filled with ice, combine the gin and vermouth. Cover, shake vigorously, and strain into a chilled martini glass. Garnish with the olive.

MARGARITA

Kosher salt for rimming glass
1 lime wedge
2 oz (60 ml) tequila blanco
1½ oz (45 ml) triple sec
1 oz (30 ml) fresh lime juice
1 lime slice

Pour the salt onto a small plate . Gently rub the lime wedge around the rim of a rocks or couple glass. Holding the base of the glass, dip the rim into the salt. Fill a cocktail shaker with ice. Add the tequila, triple sec, and lime juice. Cover, shake vigorously, and strain into the glass. Garnish with the lime slice.

STIRRED

OLD-FASHIONED

3 dashes Angostura bitters
1 orange slice
1 lemon wedge
1 maraschino cherry
1 sugar cube
2½ oz (75 ml) blended Canadia whiskey

In an old-fashioned glass, muddle the angostura bitters, orange slice, lemon wedge, maraschino cherry, and sugar cube. Fill the glass with ice cubes. Add the whiskey and stir.

NEGRONI

1 oz (30 ml) gin
1 oz (30 ml) sweet vermouth
1 oz (30 ml) Campari
1 orange slice

Fill a rocks glass with ice. Add the gin, vermouth, and Campari and stir. Garnish with the orange slice.

GIN GIMLET

2½ oz (75 ml) gin
½ oz (15 ml) sweetened lime juice, such as Rose's
1 lime wedge

Fill a rocks glass with ice. Add the gin and lime juice and stir. Garnish with the lime wedge.

MOSCOW MULE

2 oz (60 ml) vodka
1 oz (30 ml) fresh lime juice
4–6 oz (120-180 ml) ginger beer
1 lime wedge

Fill a copper mug with ice. Add the vodka, lime juice, and ginger beer and stir. Garnish with the lime wedge.

MANHATTAN

2½ oz (75 ml) rye, bourbon, or blended Canadian Whiskey
¾ oz (22 ml) sweet vermouth
2 dashes Angostura bitters
1 maraschino cherry

In a mixing glass filled with ice, combine the rye, vermouth, and bitters and stir well. Strain into a chilled martini glass. Garnish with the cherry.

BAR MIXERS

Think of cocktails as you think of food—flavor, freshness, and seasonality are key. Each element plays a big role in the final creation. Any time-honored classic is a welcome guest at cocktail hour, but by changing up one ingredient, you can transform a traditional libation into a completely new drink.

Fresh juices Fresh juice is key, especially citrus, which lends a subtle fragrance to the drink from both the juice and the rind. There are many tools available for making fresh juice at home (see page 8), but if you don't have the right one for the task, splurge on freshly squeezed juice from the store.

Aromatic bitters These flavor enhancers are made by macerating and distilling aromatic plants, spices, or citrus peel in a base of alcohol. As their name implies, they have a very bitter taste, which adds complexity to a drink. The best known are Angostura, Peychaud's, and orange bitters.

Vermouth A fortified white wine–based aperitif flavored with plants. Traditionally, sweet vermouths (amber in color) come from Italy and dry (clear in color) are from France.

Liqueurs Made from distilled spirits and from fruits or other plants, liqueurs contain less alcohol and more added sugar than liquor. Chartreuse (from herbs), maraschino liqueur (from cherries), and triple sec (from oranges) are favorites.

Simple syrup This versatile mixer (page 92) is an essential element of many cocktails for both sweetness and overall taste. Infusing simple syrups with vanilla, citrus, spices, herbs, or dried flowers can create an entirely new flavor profile for a drink.

13

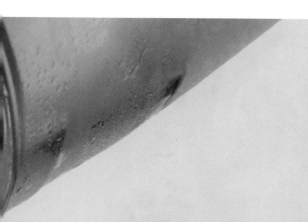

VODKA

16 Strawberry-Lillet Vodka Soda

20 Peppermint White Russian

21 Blood Orange Cosmopolitan

23 Pomegranate Martini

24 Meyer Lemon–Rosemary Moscow Mule

24 St-Germain Greyhound

STRAWBERRY-LILLET VODKA SODA

The vodka soda is a bartender's dream: vodka, soda, and ice, and that's it. But it can also be kind of boring. This recipe freshens up that familiar order, introducing muddled strawberries and Lillet, a fruity fortified wine, and gives everything a good shake.

4 STRAWBERRIES, SLICED

½ OZ (15 ML) SIMPLE SYRUP (PAGE 92)

½ OZ (15 ML) FRESH LIME JUICE

1½ OZ (45 ML) VODKA

1 OZ (30 ML) LILLET

2 OZ (60 ML) CLUB SODA

1 LIME WEDGE

Reserve 1 strawberry slice for garnish. In a cocktail shaker, muddle the remaining strawberries, simple syrup, and lime juice until the strawberries are crushed. Add the vodka, Lillet, and ice. Cover, shake vigorously, and strain into an ice-filled Collins or highball glass. Top with the club soda. Garnish with the lime wedge and reserved strawberry slice.

Simple syrup is a bar
staple, and it can be
infused with a variety
of flavors (see page 92).

Use a king cube silicone ice tray to produce blocky colossal cubes, ideal for drinks in wide, low glasses.

Tall ice cylinders add elegance to drinks served in collins glasses.

All-purpose ice cubes, from small to large, are the most common shape.

Ice spheres keep stirred cocktails cold without overdiluting them.

ON THE ROCKS

Ice is a key element in a cocktail. The size, shape, and amount you use can affect the taste of the drink—larger cubes melt slowly, preserving the flavors longer, while crushed ice melts quickly but guarantees a frosty glass. For crystal clear, bar-perfect ice at home, consider buying cubes from your favorite local watering hole.

Crushed ice, a signature for juleps and swizzles, is ideal for cocktails with strong liquors that need to be chilled quickly.

PEPPERMINT WHITE RUSSIAN

Peppermint on the rim and in the glass gives this old favorite a new flavor. Here, the half-and-half is stirred in, but some White Russian drinkers insist that it be floated on top. If you don't want to fuss with the cream, omit it and you'll have a Black Russian.

HALF-AND-HALF FOR RIMMING GLASS, PLUS 1½ OZ (45 ML)

CRUSHED PEPPERMINT CANDIES FOR RIMMING GLASS

1½ OZ (45 ML) KAHLÚA

1 OZ (30 ML) VODKA

1 OZ (30 ML) PEPPERMINT SCHNAPPS

Pour some half-and-half into a small, shallow bowl. On a small plate, spread the peppermint candies in an even layer. Holding the base of a rocks glass, dip the rim into the half-and-half and then into the candies. Place the glass in the refrigerator until ready to use.

Just before serving, fill the glass with ice. Add the coffee liqueur, vodka, and peppermint schnapps and stir to combine. Add the 1½ oz (45 ml) half-and-half and stir until blended.

BLOOD ORANGE COSMOPOLITAN

A staple of girlfriend get-togethers and parties of all kinds, the cosmopolitan sheds its signature deep red cranberry juice for the aromatic, scarlet juice of the blood orange in this updated version of the festive classic.

2 OZ (60 ML) VODKA

1 OZ (30 ML) COINTREAU

1 OZ (30 ML) FRESH BLOOD ORANGE JUICE

½ OZ (15 ML) FRESH LIME JUICE

½ OZ (15 ML) SIMPLE SYRUP (PAGE 92)

1 BLOOD ORANGE SLICE

In a cocktail shaker filled with ice, combine the vodka, Cointreau, blood orange juice, lime juice, and simple syrup. Cover, shake vigorously, and strain into a chilled martini glass. Garnish with the blood orange slice floated on top.

Pomegranate juice can vary greatly in terms of sweetness. The POM Wonderful brand yields the best results for this tart-sweet cocktail.

POMEGRANATE MARTINI

The martini has left behind its legendary simplicity in this colorful, fruit-flavored cocktail. Grand Marnier will work here in place of the Cointreau, though it is a bit sweeter and heavier, and you can skip the garnish of seeds if pomegranates are out of season.

1 OZ (30 ML) POMEGRANATE JUICE, PLUS MORE FOR RIMMING GLASS

SUGAR FOR RIMMING GLASS

2 OZ (60 ML) VODKA

½ OZ (15 ML) COINTREAU

½ OZ (15 ML) FRESH ORANGE JUICE

1 ORANGE TWIST

1 TEASPOON POMEGRANATE SEEDS

Pour some pomegranate juice into a small bowl. On a small plate, spread sugar in an even layer. Holding a martini glass by the stem, dip the rim into the pomegranate juice and then into the sugar. Refrigerate until ready to use.

In a cocktail shaker filled with ice, combine the 1 oz (30 ml) pomegranate juice, the vodka, Cointreau, and orange juice. Cover, shake vigorously, and strain into the chilled glass. Garnish with the orange twist and pomegranate seeds.

MEYER LEMON–ROSEMARY MOSCOW MULE

The Moscow mule is said to have helped put vodka on nearly every back bar in the States. In this version, Meyer lemon replaces the usual lime, and rosemary adds a light herbaceous note. A copper mug is traditional, but a rocks glass will do.

2 OZ (60 ML) VODKA

1 OZ (30 ML) FRESH MEYER LEMON JUICE

½ OZ (15 ML) ROSEMARY SIMPLE SYRUP (PAGE 92)

3 OZ (90 ML) GINGER BEER

1 FRESH ROSEMARY SPRIG

1 LEMON SLICE

In a cocktail shaker filled with ice, combine the vodka, lemon juice, and rosemary simple syrup. Cover, shake vigorously, and strain into an ice-filled copper mug. Top with the ginger beer. Garnish with the rosemary sprig and lemon slice.

SERVES 1

ST-GERMAIN GREYHOUND

The warm floral notes of St-Germain soften the tart nature of the traditional greyhound without compromising its bright, refreshing taste. Dampen the glass rim with grapefruit and coat it with salt and the Greyhound becomes a Salty Dog.

4 OZ (125 ML) FRESH GRAPEFRUIT JUICE

2 OZ (60 ML) VODKA

1 OZ (30 ML) ST-GERMAIN LIQUEUR

1 GRAPEFRUIT SLICE

In a cocktail shaker filled with ice, combine the grapefruit juice, vodka, and St-Germain. Cover, shake vigorously, and strain into an ice-filled highball glass. Garnish with the grapefruit slice.

If Meyer lemons are
hard to find, use regular
lemons but compensate
by adding a little more
simple syrup to the mix.

GIN

29 Spanish Gin & Tonic

29 Apple & Honey Bee's Knees

30 French 75 with Lavender & Lemon

30 Lemongrass Last Word

33 Grapefruit & Sage Gimlet

33 Ramos Gin Fizz

34 Lime & Thyme Gin Fizz

34 Sparkling Corpse Reviver

35 Elderflower-Rose Collins

35 Pegu Cocktail

36 Tarragon Negroni

Edible flowers offer a pretty dash of color and elegance to cocktails. Try pansies, violets, nasturtium, rose petals, or herb blossoms.

SPANISH GIN & TONIC

Don't be shy when it comes to garnishing this Spanish version of the cocktail classic. Iberian bartenders traditionally load on flowers, herbs, and spices to heighten the botanicals in the gin.

4 OZ (125 ML) TONIC WATER

2 OZ (60 ML) GIN

2 DASHES ANGOSTURA BITTERS

JUNIPER BERRIES, GRAPEFRUIT SLICE, LEMON TWIST, EDIBLE FLOWERS, AND/OR FRESH ROSEMARY

Fill a rocks glass with ice. Add the tonic, gin, and Angostura bitters and stir to combine. Garnish with juniper berries, grapefruit slice, lemon twist, edible flowers, and/or fresh herbs.

SERVES 1

APPLE & HONEY BEE'S KNEES

This modern take on the prohibition-era classic swaps out the traditional honey for sweet cinnamon-apple syrup.

1 TABLESPOON SUGAR MIXED WITH 1 TEASPOON GROUND CINNAMON

1 LEMON WEDGE

2 OZ (60 ML) GIN

1½ OZ (45 ML) CINNAMON-APPLE SYRUP (PAGE 92)

1 OZ (30 ML) FRESH LEMON JUICE

1 CINNAMON STICK

1 APPLE SLICE

Sprinkle the cinnamon-sugar on a small plate. Gently rub the lemon wedge around the rim of a coupe glass and dip it into the cinnamon sugar. In a cocktail shaker filled with ice, combine the gin, cinnamon-apple syrup, and lemon juice. Cover, shake vigorously, and strain into the glass. Garnish with the cinnamon stick and float an apple slice on top.

FRENCH 75 WITH LAVENDER & LEMON

This Champagne cocktail was named for a French field gun as the original mix was said to carry an artillery-like kick. Here, the power of the French 75 is tempered with a double dose of fragrant lavender.

1 OZ (30 ML) GIN

½ OZ (15 ML) LAVENDER SIMPLE SYRUP (PAGE 92)

½ OZ (15 ML) FRESH LEMON JUICE

2 OZ (60 ML) CHAMPAGNE OR SPARKLING WINE

2 FRESH LAVENDER SPRIGS

1 LEMON TWIST

In a cocktail shaker filled with ice, combine the gin, lavender simple syrup, and lemon juice. Cover, shake vigorously, and strain into a Champagne flute. Top with the Champagne. Garnish with the lavender sprigs and lemon twist.

LEMONGRASS LAST WORD

Two Southeast Asian flavors—lemongrass and kaffir lime—give this sweet-sour cocktail a refreshing profile. Add equal parts of all ingredients to scale up for serving a crowd.

¾ OZ (20 ML) GIN

¾ OZ (20 ML) GREEN CHARTREUSE

¾ OZ (20 ML) LEMONGRASS SIMPLE SYRUP (PAGE 92)

¾ OZ (20 ML) FRESH LIME JUICE

1 KAFFIR LIME LEAF

1 LIME WEDGE

In a cocktail shaker filled with ice, combine the gin, green Chartreuse, lemongrass simple syrup, and lime juice. Cover, shake vigorously, and strain into a chilled coupe glass. Garnish with the kaffir lime leaf and lime wedge.

A tall sprig of fresh
lavender does double duty
as fragrant garnish and
Champagne swizzle stick.

Fresh sage and tart
grapefruit are refreshing
and complementary
partners in the glass.

GRAPEFRUIT & SAGE GIMLET

In this gimlet redux, tangy grapefruit juice replaces the traditional lemon juice, and sage is added to impart an herbaceous flavor.

2½ OZ (70 ML) GIN

1 OZ (30 ML) FRESH GRAPEFRUIT JUICE

½ OZ (15 ML) SAGE SIMPLE SYRUP (PAGE 92)

1 GRAPEFRUIT SLICE

1 FRESH SAGE LEAF

In a cocktail shaker filled with ice, combine the gin, grapefruit juice, and sage simple syrup. Cover, shake vigorously, and strain into an ice-filled rocks glass. Garnish with the grapefruit slice and sage leaf.

RAMOS GIN FIZZ

A sprinkling of freshly grated nutmeg is the classic finish to this iconic cocktail. A twist of orange garnish, as here, brightens the overall flavor.

2 OZ (60 ML) GIN

2 OZ (60 ML) SIMPLE SYRUP (PAGE 92)

½ OZ (15 ML) HALF-AND-HALF

½ OZ (15 ML) FRESH LEMON JUICE

½ OZ (15 ML) FRESH LIME JUICE

1 DASH ORANGE BLOSSOM WATER

1 LARGE EGG WHITE

1 OZ (30 ML) SELTZER WATER

1 ORANGE TWIST

In a cocktail shaker, combine the gin, simple syrup, half-and-half, lemon juice, lime juice, orange blossom water, and egg white. Cover and shake well. Add ice. Shake again, and strain into a rocks glass. Top with the seltzer water. Garnish with the orange twist.

LIME & THYME GIN FIZZ

Thyme gives this gin fizz a unique accent. For a silver fizz, add an egg white to the cocktail shaker; for a golden fizz, add a whole egg.

2 OZ (60 ML) GIN

½ OZ (15 ML) FRESH LIME JUICE

½ OZ (15 ML) THYME SIMPLE SYRUP (PAGE 92)

2 OZ (60 ML) CLUB SODA

1 LIME SLICE

2 FRESH THYME SPRIGS

In a cocktail shaker filled with ice, combine the gin, lime juice, and thyme simple syrup. Cover, shake vigorously, and strain into an ice-filled rocks glass. Top with the club soda. Garnish with the lime slice and thyme sprigs floated on the top.

SERVES 1

SPARKLING CORPSE REVIVER

This gin-based cocktail is one of the best-known members of this family of hangover cures. A splash of club soda speeds the recovery.

¾ OZ (20 ML) GIN

¾ OZ (20 ML) LILLET

½ OZ (15 ML) COINTREAU

½ OZ (15 ML) FRESH LEMON JUICE

1 DASH ABSINTHE

1 OZ CLUB SODA

1 LUXARDO MARASCHINO CHERRY

In a cocktail shaker filled with ice, combine the gin, Lillet, Cointreau, lemon juice, and absinthe. Cover, shake vigorously, and strain into a chilled coupe glass. Top with the club soda and garnish with the maraschino cherry.

SERVES 1

ELDERFLOWER-ROSE COLLINS

The Tom Collins, an iconic gentleman's drink, gets a flowery infusion with rose-scented simple syrup and elderflower liqueur.

2 OZ (60 ML) GIN

1 OZ (30 ML) FRESH LEMON JUICE

½ OZ (15 ML) ROSE SIMPLE SYRUP (PAGE 92)

3 OZ (80 ML) CLUB SODA

½ OZ (15 ML) ST-GERMAIN LIQUEUR

1 LEMON TWIST

1 EDIBLE FLOWER

In a cocktail shaker filled with ice, combine the gin, lemon juice, and rose simple syrup. Cover, shake vigorously, and strain into an ice-filled highball glass. Top with the club soda and St-Germain and stir. Garnish with the lemon twist and flower.

SERVES 1

PEGU COCKTAIL

This cocktail was named for the Pegu Club, a British men's club once located just outside Rangoon, Burma (today Yangon, Myanmar).

2 OZ (60 ML) GIN

¾ OZ (20 ML) COINTREAU

½ OZ (15 ML) FRESH LIME JUICE

¼ OZ (7 ML) FRESH ORANGE JUICE

3 DASHES ANGOSTURA BITTERS

2 DASHES ORANGE BITTERS

1 LIME SLICE

In a cocktail shaker filled with ice, combine the gin, Cointreau, lime juice, orange juice, Angostura bitters, and orange bitters. Cover, shake vigorously, and strain into a chilled martini glass. Garnish with the lime slice.

TARRAGON NEGRONI

In this riff on the edgy, strong Italian aperitif, the traditional sweet vermouth has been swapped out in favor of Bordeaux-based Lillet. Bittersweet Peychaud's and anise-scented tarragon finish the already heady mix.

2 OZ (60 ML) GIN

1 OZ (30 ML) CAMPARI

1 OZ (30 ML) LILLET

1 OZ (30 ML) FRESH LEMON JUICE

¼ OZ (7 ML) TARRAGON SIMPLE SYRUP (PAGE 92)

1 DASH PEYCHAUD'S BITTERS

1 FRESH TARRAGON SPRIG

In a cocktail shaker filled with ice, combine the gin, Campari, Lillet, lemon juice, tarragon simple syrup, and Peychaud's bitters. Cover, shake vigorously, and strain into a chilled rocks or coupe glass. Add ice if desired and garnish with the tarragon sprig.

Anise-scented tarragon and Campari are a fragrant blend. Add to the flavorful mélange with an orange twist, if you like.

RUM

41 Mango Mai Tai

44 Mint Hemingway Daiquiri

45 Gingerbread Dark & Stormy

46 Rosemary-Ginger Mojito

Temper the mai tai's signature sweet fruitiness with a handful of salted Tamari-Maple Mixed Nuts (page 88).

MANGO MAI TAI

The mai tai makes nearly everyone dream of a sun-drenched sandy beach, but this fruit-laden rum-based drink will taste good in your living room, too. If you can find paper cocktail umbrellas, slide them into the glasses alongside the garnishes.

4 CUPS (640 G) RIPE MANGO CHUNKS

¼ CUP (50 G) SUGAR

1 CUP (250 ML) DARK RUM

1 CUP (250 ML) PINEAPPLE JUICE

½ CUP (125 ML) SIMPLE SYRUP (PAGE 92)

4 TABLESPOONS GRENADINE

4 FRESH PINEAPPLE WEDGES

4 MARASCHINO CHERRIES

In a blender, combine the mango, sugar, and ¼ cup (60 ml) water and blend until smooth and no chunks of mango remain. Add the rum, pineapple juice, and simple syrup and blend until thoroughly combined. Pour the contents of the blender into 4 ice-filled tall wine glasses and top each drink with 1 tablespoon grenadine. Garnish each mai tai with a pineapple wedge and a maraschino cherry.

Citrus Wedges

Mint Sprig

Rosemary

Lemon Twist

Flowering
Thyme Sprigs

GARNISHES
GALORE

Garnishes are an opportunity to layer
flavors and put a stylish finishing
touch on a drink. Be creative and
add your own signature flair.

Rimming Sugar
with Lime Zest
(Page 64)

Lavender

Anise Flowers

Cocktail Picks

Pineapple

Pomegranate Seeds

Strawberries

Edible Blossoms

Currants

Blackberries

Cherries

MINT HEMINGWAY DAIQUIRI

First mixed in Cuba and now enjoyed around the world, the basic daiquiri is made from white rum, lime juice, and sugar. The Hemingway drops the sugar, ups the rum and lime juice, and adds grapefruit and maraschino liqueur. Here, the mint is muddled in the shaker for an added hit of fresh herbal flavor.

¼ CUP (¼ OZ/15 G) FRESH MINT LEAVES

2 OZ (60 ML) LIGHT RUM

¾ OZ (20 ML) FRESH LIME JUICE

½ OZ (15 ML) FRESH GRAPEFRUIT JUICE

½ OZ (15 ML) MARASCHINO LIQUEUR

1 FRESH MINT SPRIG

1 LIME SLICE

In a cocktail shaker, muddle the mint leaves, rum, lime juice, grapefruit juice, and maraschino liqueur until the mint is aromatic. Fill the shaker with ice, cover, shake vigorously, and strain into an ice-filled coupe glass. Place the mint sprig in the center of the lime slice and float on top of the drink.

GINGERBREAD DARK & STORMY

Gingerbread simple syrup gives this seafarer's drink from Bermuda a more complex flavor, playing off the caramel overtones of the dark rum and the spicy kick of the ginger beer. Traditionalists use Bermuda's own Gosling's Black Seal rum.

2 OZ (60 ML) DARK RUM

¾ OZ (20 ML) FRESH LIME JUICE

½ OZ (15 ML) GINGERBREAD SIMPLE SYRUP (PAGE 92)

3 OZ (90 ML) GINGER BEER

1 CINNAMON STICK

1 SLICE CRYSTALLIZED GINGER

In a chilled highball glass, combine the rum, lime juice, and gingerbread syrup. Add ice and stir. Top with the ginger beer and more ice. Garnish with the cinnamon stick and crystallized ginger.

ROSEMARY-GINGER MOJITO

This modern take on the Cuban national cocktail adds ginger and rosemary to the classic minty mix—a fragrant and flavorful partnership that pairs perfectly with the vanilla tones of the rum. To release more flavor from the rosemary sprig, lightly bruise it before slipping it into the glass.

2 OZ (60 G) CRYSTALLIZED GINGER

½ CUP (100 G) SUGAR

1 LIME WEDGE

10 FRESH MINT LEAVES

2 OZ (60 ML) WHITE RUM

1 OZ (30 ML) FRESH LIME JUICE

½ OZ (15 ML) ROSEMARY-GINGER SIMPLE SYRUP (PAGE 92)

1 OZ (30 ML) CLUB SODA

1 FRESH MINT SPRIG

1 FRESH ROSEMARY SPRIG

In a mini food processor, combine the crystallized ginger and sugar and pulse until finely ground. Pour the ginger-sugar mixture onto a small plate and spread in an even layer. Gently rub the lime wedge around the rim of a highball glass. Holding the base of the glass, dip the rim into the ginger-sugar mixture. Refrigerate until ready to use.

Just before serving, fill the glass with ice. In a cocktail shaker, muddle the mint leaves. Add the rum, lime juice, rosemary-ginger simple syrup, and ice. Cover, shake vigorously, and strain into the ice-filled glass. Top with the club soda and garnish with the mint and rosemary sprigs.

For an extra burst of sweetness, run a lime wedge along the rim of the glass and dip it in sugar before pouring in the cocktail.

WHISKEY & BOURBON

51   Hibiscus & Tart Cherry Manhattan

51   Smoky Maple Sazerac

52   Basil Julep

55   Blackberry Lemonade Whiskey Sour

55   Vanilla-Citrus Old-Fashioned

Dress up oversized ice cubes with fresh or frozen cherries (see page 93). Silicon trays work best for these specialty sizes.

HIBISCUS & TART CHERRY MANHATTAN

The classic trio of whiskey, vermouth, and aromatic bitters is a bar favorite—made modern here with the rich flavors of hibiscus and cherry. Rye whiskey is typically preferred, but any type will do.

2 OZ (60 ML) WHISKEY

½ OZ (15 ML) SWEET VERMOUTH

½ OZ (15 ML) HIBISCUS SIMPLE SYRUP (PAGE 13)

2 DASHES ANGOSTURA BITTERS

1 CHERRY ICE CUBE (PAGE 93)

In a mixing glass, combine the whiskey, sweet vermouth, hibiscus simple syrup, and Angostura bitters. Add regular ice and stir well until chilled. Place the cherry ice cube in a rocks glass and strain the contents of the mixing glass into the rocks glass.

SERVES 1

SMOKY MAPLE SAZERAC

This updated Sazerac gets its sweet edge from maple syrup rather than a crushed sugar cube. A hint of smokiness adds a welcome twist.

¼ (7 ML) OZ ABSINTHE

2 OZ (60 ML) RYE WHISKEY

½ OZ (15 ML) GRADE A PURE MAPLE SYRUP

3 DASHES LIQUID SMOKE

3 DASHES PEYCHAUD'S BITTERS

1 LEMON TWIST

Pour the absinthe into a rocks glass and swirl to coat the sides. Add 1 large ice cube. Set aside. In a cocktail shaker filled with ice, combine the rye whiskey, maple syrup, liquid smoke, and Peychaud's bitters. Cover and shake vigorously. Discard the ice and absinthe from the glass. Strain the contents of the cocktail shaker into the glass and garnish with the lemon twist.

BASIL JULEP

Basil stands in for the mint in this contemporary version of the Southern classic. Julep fans and Kentucky Derby–goers alike will appreciate this makeover, which mixes the pungent basil and tart lime with a top-shelf bourbon. Don't skimp on the crushed ice—it is essential to a good julep.

9 FRESH BASIL LEAVES

1 OZ (30 ML) BASIL SIMPLE SYRUP (PAGE 92)

1½ OZ (45 ML) BOURBON

1 OZ (30 ML) FRESH LIME JUICE

1 LIME WEDGE

In a rocks glass, muddle 8 of the basil leaves and the basil simple syrup. Add the bourbon and lime juice, pack the glass tightly with crushed ice, and stir until the glass is frosted on the outside. Top with more crushed ice to form a dome. Garnish with the remaining basil leaf and the lime wedge.

Silver julep cups are the traditional way to serve this refreshing cocktail, but clear glass tumblers ensure a lovely view of the crushed basil inside.

For easy mixing, freeze the leftover blackberry coulis in an ice cube tray for up to 4 months. Thaw a cube and add to the shaker whenever a hankering for this fruity sour hits.

BLACKBERRY LEMONADE WHISKEY SOUR

This dressed-up version of a whiskey sour adds sweet blackberry coulis to the traditional mix of whiskey, lemon juice, and sugar.

2 OZ (60 ML) WHISKEY

1½ OZ (45 ML) FRESH LEMON JUICE

1 OZ (30 ML) SIMPLE SYRUP (PAGE 92)

1 OZ (30 ML) BLACKBERRY COULIS (PAGE 93)

1 LARGE EGG WHITE

1 LEMON TWIST

In a cocktail shaker, combine the whiskey, lemon juice, simple syrup, blackberry coulis, and egg white. Cover and shake vigorously, then open the shaker and add ice. Cover, shake vigorously again, and strain into a chilled rocks glass over 1 large ice cube. Garnish with the lemon twist.

SERVES 1

VANILLA-CITRUS OLD-FASHIONED

The addition of vanilla heightens similar notes in the whiskey, and the extra dose of citrus gives this cocktail classic a brighter flavor.

1-INCH (2.5-CM) PIECE VANILLA BEAN, PLUS 1 VANILLA BEAN FOR GARNISH

2-INCH (5-CM) PIECE LEMON PEEL

2-INCH (5-CM) PIECE ORANGE PEEL

¼ OZ (7 G) VANILLA SIMPLE SYRUP (PAGE 92)

3 DASHES ORANGE BITTERS

2 OZ (60 ML) BOURBON

SQUEEZE OF FRESH ORANGE JUICE (OPTIONAL)

1 ORANGE TWIST

In a rocks glass, muddle the vanilla bean, lemon peel, orange peel, simple syrup, and orange bitters. Add 1 large ice cube and the bourbon, and stir gently. Top with the orange juice, if using. Garnish with the vanilla bean and orange twist.

TEQUILA

58   Cranberry-Tequila Punch

61   Tequila Sunrise with Pineapple & Jalapeño

62   Tequila & Ancho Reyes with Cucumber

63   Tarragon Paloma

64   Coconut Cream & Lime Margarita

CRANBERRY-TEQUILA PUNCH

A fruit-filled ice ring made from apple and cranberry juices keeps this sparkling punch cool without diluting its flavor. You can use a mix of citrus slices—lemon, lime, blood orange—instead of only orange, or you can use apple slices in place of the citrus.

6 CUPS (1.5 L) APPLE JUICE, CHILLED

6 CUPS (1.5 L) LOW-SUGAR CRANBERRY COCKTAIL, CHILLED

1 LARGE ORANGE, HALVED LENGTHWISE, THEN THINLY SLICED CROSSWISE

1 CUP (100 G) FRESH OR FROZEN CRANBERRIES

2 CUPS (500 ML) REPOSADO TEQUILA

1 CUP (250 ML) ORANGE LIQUEUR, SUCH AS GRAND MARNIER OR COINTREAU

2 BOTTLES (750 ML EACH) SPARKLING WINE, SUCH AS PROSECCO

18 FRESH ROSEMARY SPRIGS, EACH THREADED WITH 3 CRANBERRIES

To make the ice ring, pour 1 cup (250 ml) of the apple juice and 1 cup of the cranberry cocktail into an 8- or 9-inch (20- or 23-cm) Bundt pan or ring mold. Add half of the orange slices in a single layer, then half of the cranberries. Freeze until firm, at least 3 hours. Add the remaining orange slices and cranberries to the mold. Fill with 1 cup of the apple juice and 1 cup of the cranberry cocktail. Freeze until solid, at least 3 hours.

In a large bowl or pitcher, stir together the remaining 4 cups (1 kg) apple juice, 4 cups cranberry cocktail, the tequila, orange liqueur, and sparkling wine. Remove the ring mold from the freezer and invert onto a plate. Run the bottom of the mold under warm water until the ice ring releases. Slide the ice ring, fruit side up, into a large punch bowl. Fill the bowl with the punch.

To serve, ladle the punch into rocks or coupe glasses and garnish each with a cranberry-threaded rosemary sprig.

Punch is the perfect party companion. Prepare the ice ring ahead of time and add it to the punch bowl just before guests arrive.

A subtle infusion of
jalapeño chile and
caramelized pineapple
add unexpected heat
and depth of flavor
to this riff on the
cocktail classic.

TEQUILA SUNRISE WITH PINEAPPLE & JALAPEÑO

With it's crimson to golden hue and fruity flavor, this ombre cocktail is a favorite party drink. Here, the classic mix is given a contemporary spin with muddled chile and charred pineapple. For a tequila sunset, substitute blackberry brandy for the grenadine.

2 OZ (60 ML) PINEAPPLE CHUNKS

4 THIN SLICES JALAPEÑO CHILE

4 OZ (125 ML) FRESH ORANGE JUICE

2 OZ (60 ML) TEQUILA

½ OZ (15 ML) GRENADINE

Pat the pineapple chunks dry on a paper towel. In a small frying pan over medium-high heat, cook the pineapple, turning once, until beginning to char, about 3 minutes per side. Remove from the heat and let cool briefly. Reserve 1 chunk for garnish.

In a cocktail shaker, muddle the remaining pineapple chunks and 3 of the jalapeño slices. Add the orange juice, tequila, and ice. Cover, shake vigorously, and strain into an ice-filled highball glass. Slowly pour the grenadine over the back of a spoon into the glass. Garnish with the reserved pineapple chunk and the remaining jalapeño slice.

TEQUILA & ANCHO REYES WITH CUCUMBER

Spicy, sweet, and faintly smoky, Ancho Reyes is a high-octane chile liqueur made in Puebla, Mexico, by steeping the local ancho chiles in a sugarcane-based spirit. If you can't find Ancho Reyes, increase the tequila to 1½ oz (45 ml) and add 2 dashes firewater bitters.

KOSHER SALT, SUGAR, AND CHILI POWDER FOR RIMMING GLASS

2 LIME WEDGES

1½ OZ (45 ML) FRESH LIME JUICE

1 OZ (30 ML) ANCHO REYES LIQUEUR

1 OZ (30 ML) TEQUILA

1 OZ (30 ML) CUCUMBER JUICE (PAGE 93)

½ OZ (15 ML) AGAVE SYRUP (PAGE 93)

1 CUCUMBER SLICE

On a small plate, mix equal parts salt and sugar to ½ part chili powder and spread in an even layer. Gently rub 1 of the lime wedges around half of the rim and partway down the side of a rocks glass. Holding the base of the glass, dip the moistened rim and side into the salt mixture. Refrigerate until ready to use.

Just before serving, fill the glass with ice. In a cocktail shaker filled with ice, combine the lime juice, Ancho Reyes, tequila, cucumber juice, and agave syrup. Cover, shake vigorously, and strain into the ice-filled glass. Garnish with the cucumber slice.

Just before serving, fill the glass with ice. In a cocktail shaker filled with ice, combine the coconut cream, tequila, lime juice, Cointreau, and simple syrup. Cover, shake vigorously, and strain into the ice-filled glass. Garnish with the remaining lime wedge.

TARRAGON PALOMA

Choose a good blanco tequila—or a reposado if you prefer a richer flavor—for this refreshing tequila cocktail. For a fizzier drink, mix as directed, skipping the fresh grapefruit juice and club soda to top off the glass with grapefruit soda (look for Jarritos brand from Mexico).

KOSHER SALT

2 GRAPEFRUIT WEDGES

3 FRESH TARRAGON SPRIGS

2 OZ (60 ML) TEQUILA

2 OZ (60 ML) FRESH GRAPEFRUIT JUICE

½ OZ (15 ML) FRESH LIME JUICE

½ OZ (15 ML) TARRAGON SIMPLE SYRUP (PAGE 92)

1 OZ (30 ML) CLUB SODA

On a small plate, spread salt in an even layer. Gently rub 1 of the grapefruit wedges around the rim of a highball glass. Holding the base of the glass, dip the rim into the salt. Refrigerate until ready to use.

Just before serving, fill the glass with ice. In a cocktail shaker, muddle 2 of the tarragon sprigs. Add the tequila, grapefruit juice, lime juice, tarragon simple syrup, and ice. Cover, shake vigorously, and strain into the ice-filled glass. Top with the club soda. Garnish with the remaining grapefruit wedge and tarragon sprig.

COCONUT CREAM & LIME MARGARITA

Blanco tequila is a pure form of the agave-fermeneted alcohol which, unlike resposados and añejos, is not aged in wood. Here, the lightest tequila gets a rich and creamy edge from coconut cream, to which the standard mix of orange-flavored liqueur and lime juice is added.

KOSHER SALT, GRATED LIME ZEST, AND SUGAR FOR RIMMING GLASS

2 LIME WEDGES

2 OZ (60 ML) COCONUT CREAM OR CREAM OF COCONUT

1½ OZ (45 ML) BLANCO TEQUILA

1 OZ (30 ML) FRESH LIME JUICE

½ OZ (15 ML) COINTREAU

¼ OZ (7 ML) SIMPLE SYRUP (PAGE 92)

On a small plate, combine equal parts salt, lime zest, and sugar and spread in an even layer. Gently rub 1 of the lime wedges around the rim of a rocks glass. Holding the base of the glass, dip the rim into the salt mixture. Place in the refrigerator until ready to use.

Just before serving, fill the glass with ice. In a cocktail shaker filled with ice, combine the coconut cream, tequila, lime juice, Cointreau, and simple syrup. Cover, shake vigorously, and strain into the ice-filled glass. Garnish with the remaining lime wedge.

This creamy margarita
is a hit when made in the
blender too. Quadruple
the recipe and serve
from a pitcher.

SPECIALTY

69   Rosé Sangria with Citrus and Raspberries

70   Sparkling Lemon & Raspberry Float

70   Strawberry-Basil Mimosa

75   Blackberry-Thyme Bellini

75   Lychee & Lime Sake Cocktail

76   Piña Colada Ice Pops

76   Amaretto Affogato

78   Hard Watermelon Lemonade

79   Raspberry-Peach Frozen Daiquiri

81   Salted Caramel Irish Coffee

81   Apple-Spice Hot Toddy

Try any of your favorite fruits in this updated version of the Spanish classic. Sliced stone fruits and fresh blackberries also partner well with rosé.

ROSÉ SANGRIA WITH CITRUS & RASPBERRIES

Traditionally made with red or white wine, this Spanish staple is updated with rosé wine, fresh grapefruit juice, and fresh raspberries. For a less potent sangria, add more juice.

1 BOTTLE (750 ML) ROSÉ WINE

1 CUP (250 ML) FRESH GRAPEFRUIT JUICE

½ CUP (125 ML) FRESH ORANGE JUICE

3 OZ (90 ML) COINTREAU

3 OZ (90 ML) BRANDY

2 OZ (60 ML) SIMPLE SYRUP (PAGE 92)

1 SMALL LEMON, CUT INTO ½-INCH (6-MM) SLICES

1 ORANGE, CUT INTO ½-INCH (6-MM) SLICES

4 CUPS (450 G) RASPBERRIES

¾ CUP (180 ML) SODA WATER

In a large pitcher, combine the wine, grapefruit juice, orange juice, Cointreau, brandy, and simple syrup and stir until blended. Stir in the lemon and orange slices and the raspberries. Refrigerate for at least 1 hour or up to 8 hours.

Pour the soda water into the sangria and stir to combine. Pour the sangria into ice-filled wine glasses.

SPARKLING LEMON & RASPBERRY FLOAT

Limoncello is a popular Italian lemon liqueur that is often served chilled as an after-dinner digestif. Here, it is balanced by sweet raspberry sorbet and fresh raspberries for an indulgent drink that could easily be served as a dessert.

¼ CUP (60 G) RASPBERRY SORBET

½ OZ (15 ML) LIMONCELLO

2 OZ (60 ML) CHILLED SPARKLING WINE

2 LEMON SLICES

3 FRESH RASPBERRIES

Place the sorbet in a wine glass or coupe glass. Pour the limoncello over the sorbet, followed by the sparkling wine. Garnish with the lemon slices and raspberries and serve with a spoon.

SERVES 1

STRAWBERRY-BASIL MIMOSA

A strawberry- and basil-infused simple syrup adds a sweet, herbal note to sparkling wine. Serve this refreshing Champagne cocktail at brunch or a summer outdoor gathering when strawberries are at their peak, dropping a berry into the glass alongside the basil sprig.

6 OZ (180 ML) CHILLED CHAMPAGNE OR SPARKLING WINE

1 OZ (30 ML) STRAWBERRY-BASIL SYRUP (PAGE 92)

1 FRESH BASIL SPRIG

In a Champagne flute or coupe glass, combine 2 oz (60 ml) of the Champagne and the strawberry-basil syrup and stir gently. Top with the remaining 4 oz (125 ml) Champagne and garnish with the basil sprig.

To chill a glass quickly, fill it with ice and cold water and let stand for a few minutes, then pour out the contents just before using.

Meyer Lemon–Rosemary
Moscow Mule
(Page 24)

Classic Dry Martini
(Page 12)

COCKTAIL PARTY

Invite friends over for an impromptu gathering where cocktails are the guests of honor. Serve an assortment of drinks with a common theme, or a mix of modern and classic libations, and pair them with a tempting selection of savory snacks. See pages 82–91 for our favorite bar bites.

Rosé Sangria
with Citrus &
Raspberries
(Page 69)

Mint
Hemingway
Daiquiri
(Page 44)

To achieve a pretty ombre effect, pour the thyme simple syrup into the flutes and fill with the Prosecco, then add the blackberry-thyme syrup.

BLACKBERRY-THYME BELLINI

Originally a mix of peach purée and Champagne, this classic Italian cocktail from Harry's Bar in Venice has taken on numerous flavor infusions since its inception in 1948. The contemporary addition of blackberry and thyme lives up to the cocktail's stylish beginnings.

3 OZ (90 ML) BLACKBERRY-THYME SYRUP (PAGE 92)

1½ OZ (45 ML) THYME SIMPLE SYRUP (PAGE 92)

1 BOTTLE (750 ML) CHILLED PROSECCO OR OTHER SPARKLING WINE

6 FRESH BLACKBERRIES

6 FRESH THYME SPRIGS

In each of 6 Champagne flutes, combine ½ oz (15 ml) blackberry-thyme syrup and ¼ oz (7 ml) thyme simple syrup. Top off each flute with 4 oz (125 ml) of the Prosecco. Garnish each Bellini with 1 blackberry and 1 thyme sprig.

LYCHEE & LIME SAKE COCKTAIL

Rice wine is a nice, light spirit for mixing, delicately accepting the flavors of the ingredients with which it is blended. Here, it melds well with sweet lychee and tart lime for a delicious drink any day of the year.

2 OZ (60 ML) SAKE

1 OZ (30 ML) LYCHEE SYRUP, STRAINED FROM THE CAN, PLUS 2 LYCHEES

1 OZ (30 ML) FRESH LIME JUICE

½ OZ (15 ML) GRENADINE

In a cocktail shaker filled with ice, combine the sake, lychee syrup, lime juice, and grenadine. Cover, shake vigorously, and strain into a chilled coupe or martini glass. Garnish with the lychees.

PIÑA COLADA ICE POPS

Take this beach-vacation favorite to the next level by freezing it in ice pop molds for a show-stopping spiked summer dessert. Omit the rum for a kid-friendly version.

2 CUPS (375 G) DICED FRESH PINEAPPLE

⅔ CUP (160 ML) COCONUT RUM, SUCH AS MALIBU

1 CAN (13.5 OZ/400 ML) COCONUT MILK, SOLIDS ONLY

1½ OZ (45 ML) SIMPLE SYRUP (PAGE 92)

10-20 MARASCHINO CHERRIES, STEMMED

In a blender, combine the pineapple, coconut rum, coconut milk solids, and simple syrup and blend until smooth. Pour the contents of the blender into 5-7 ice pop molds and add 2-3 cherries to each mold. Insert an ice pop stick into each one and freeze until firm, at least 4 hours or up to 2 weeks. Let stand at room temperature for 5 minutes, then remove the ice pops from the molds.

SERVES 1

AMARETTO AFFOGATO

The word *affogato* means "drowned" in Italian. Here, the traditional scoop of vanilla ice cream is swamped in both espresso and amaretto, resulting in an especially flavorful rendition of this classic dessert.

½ CUP (125 ML) VANILLA ICE CREAM OR GELATO

½ OZ (15 ML) AMARETTO

1 SHOT ESPRESSO OR 1½ OZ (45 ML) FRESHLY BREWED HOT COFFEE

1 ALMOND BISCOTTI, CRUMBLED

Place the ice cream in a cup or small bowl. Pour the amaretto over the ice cream, followed by the espresso. Sprinkle the biscotti pieces on top. Serve with a spoon.

Try these spiked ice pops using fresh pitted cherries for a mix of colors and flavors. You can also use fresh berries or extra chunks of pineapple for taste variations.

HARD WATERMELON LEMONADE

For a festive presentation, serve the lemonade from a large hollowed-out watermelon, using a ladle to the scoop it into the glasses. Or skip the glasses, slip straws into the watermelon bowl, and invite everyone to pull up a chair.

8 CUPS (2½ LB/1.25 KG) CUBED SEEDLESS WATERMELON

2 CUPS (500 ML) VODKA

1½ CUPS (375 ML) FRESH LEMON JUICE

1 CUP (200 G) SUGAR

8–10 LEMON SLICES

8–10 FRESH MINT SPRIGS

In a blender, combine the watermelon and 1 cup (250 ml) water and blend until smooth. Strain the mixture through a fine-mesh sieve into a bowl, discarding the solids, and return the watermelon juice to the blender. Add the vodka, lemon juice, and sugar and blend on medium speed until thoroughly combined, about 30 seconds. Pour the contents of the blender into 8–10 ice-filled highball glasses. Garnish each cocktail with a lemon slice and a mint sprig.

VARIATION: For frozen lemonade, combine 1 cup (250 ml) hard pink watermelon lemonade and 4 cups (1 kg) ice in a blender and blend on high speed until the ice is crushed and the mixture is slushy.

RASPBERRY-PEACH FROZEN DAIQUIRI

Blend up a double batch of this warm-weather refresher for your next alfresco party. You can easily replace the rum with coconut water for a virgin daiquiri.

CRUSHED FREEZE-DRIED RASPBERRIES FOR RIMMING GLASSES

1 LIME WEDGE

1½ CUPS (185 G) FROZEN RASPBERRIES

1 CUP (185 G) FROZEN PEACHES

4–6 ICE CUBES

¾ CUP (180 ML) COCONUT RUM

½ CUP (125 ML) FRESH LIME JUICE

6 TABLESPOONS (80 G) SUGAR, PLUS MORE TO TASTE

4 FRESH RASPBERRIES

4 PEACH SLICES

On a small plate, spread crushed freeze-dried raspberries in an even layer. Gently rub the lime wedge around the rim of a wine glass or coupe glass. Holding the base of the glass, dip the rim into the crushed raspberries. Repeat with 3 more glasses. Refrigerate until ready to use.

In a blender, combine the frozen raspberries and peaches, ice, coconut rum, lime juice, and sugar and blend on high speed until thoroughly combined, about 45 seconds. Taste and add more sugar, if desired. Pour the contents of the blender into the chilled glasses. Garnish each daiquiri with a fresh raspberry and a peach slice.

A double dose of salted
caramel results in an
especially rich and
buttery rendition
of this Irish classic.

SALTED CARAMEL IRISH COFFEE

One of the best antidotes to a winter's day, Irish Coffee takes on a rich, caramel sweetness in this updated version of the Gaelic favorite.

1 CUP (250 ML) FRESHLY BREWED HOT COFFEE

2 OZ (60 ML) BAILEYS IRISH CREAM

2 TABLESPOONS SALTED CARAMEL (PAGE 93), PLUS MORE FOR SERVING

WHIPPED CREAM, FOR SERVING

FLAKY SEA SALT, FOR SPRINKLING

In a large mug, combine the coffee, Baileys Irish Cream, and salted caramel and stir until the caramel is completely melted. Top with whipped cream, drizzle with the salted caramel, and sprinkle with sea salt.

SERVES 4

APPLE-SPICE HOT TODDY

The addition of cinnamon-apple syrup to this classic cold-weather cocktail enhances the rich, warming flavors.

1 CUP (250 ML) CINNAMON-APPLE SYRUP (PAGE 92)

1 CUP (250 ML) BOURBON

½ CUP (125 ML) FRESH LEMON JUICE

1 CINNAMON STICK

HONEY, TO TASTE

4 LEMON SLICES

32 WHOLE CLOVES

In a saucepan over medium-low heat, combine the cinnamon-apple syrup, bourbon, lemon juice, cinnamon stick, and 2 cups (500 ml) water. Bring to a simmer and cook, stirring occasionally, for 15 minutes to deepen the flavor. Taste, and adjust the sweetness with honey. Stud each lemon slice with 8 cloves. Divide the hot toddy among 4 mugs and garnish each drink with a clove-studded lemon slice.

BAR SNACKS

BROWN BUTTER & ROSEMARY POPCORN

The next time you make a batch of this popular bar snack, warm the butter until it is toasty brown and infuse it with fresh rosemary to create a nutty, piney flavor combo that is immediately addictive.

6 TABLESPOONS (90 G) UNSALTED BUTTER

1 TABLESPOON CHOPPED FRESH ROSEMARY

1½ TABLESPOONS CANOLA OIL

½ CUP (100 G) POPCORN KERNELS

KOSHER SALT

In a small saucepan over medium heat, melt the butter. Reduce the heat to medium-low and simmer gently, swirling the pan often, until the butter is toasty brown and smells nutty, about 5 minutes. Watch carefully at the end to prevent the butter from burning. Remove from the heat and stir in the rosemary.

In a large, heavy-bottomed saucepan over medium heat, warm the oil. Add the popcorn kernels, cover, and cook, shaking the pan occasionally, until the popping slows, about 5 minutes. Remove from the heat and wait for the popping to subside before removing the lid.

Drizzle the brown butter over the popcorn and toss to coat. Season with salt and toss again.

CITRUS & HERB MARINATED OLIVES

A myriad of fresh herbs and citrus flavors come together for a Mediterranean-inspired marinade that melds perfectly with a colorful assortment of olives.

2 CUPS (¾ LB/340 G) ASSORTED OLIVES SUCH AS NIÇOISE, CASTELVETRANO, AND KALAMATA

6 STRIPS ORANGE PEEL, EACH 3 INCHES (7.5 CM) LONG

4 STRIPS LEMON PEEL, EACH 3 INCHES (7.5 CM) LONG

¾ CUP (180 ML) OLIVE OIL

1 TABLESPOON FRESH LEMON JUICE

1 TABLESPOON FRESH ORANGE JUICE

3 CLOVES GARLIC, SMASHED

4 FRESH ROSEMARY SPRIGS

4 FRESH THYME SPRIGS

1 BAY LEAF

½ TEASPOON FENNEL SEEDS

¼ TEASPOON RED PEPPER FLAKES

In a saucepan over medium heat, combine all the ingredients. Cook until the oil begins to sizzle, about 2 minutes. Reduce the heat to low and continue to cook until the olives are just warmed through, about 5 minutes longer.

Let the olives stand at room temperature for at least 1 hour before serving to allow the flavors to blend. Alternatively, transfer the olives to a large jar, cover, and refrigerate for up to 2 weeks. Bring to room temperature or warm on the stovetop before serving.

Spanish Gin & Tonic
(Page 29)

Parmesan Straws
(Page 87)

Carrot Fries
with Granch
(Page 86)

FESTIVE FARE

With a few simple and stylish snacks,
you can throw together a gathering
with ease—no fancy clothes required!
A mix of hot and cold snacks will keep
guests satisfied and fortified.

Citrus & Herb
Marinated Olives
(Page 83)

Brown Butter &
Rosemary Popcorn
(Page 82)

Lime & Thyme Gin Fizz
(Page 34)

CARROT FRIES WITH GRANCH

Granch, short for Greek yogurt and ranch dressing, makes a zesty dip for these crispy fries coated with a tempting combination of panko, fresh parsley, and grated Parmesan cheese.

6 LARGE CARROTS, PEELED AND CUT INTO 4-BY-½-INCH (10 CM-BY-12-MM) STICKS

¼ CUP (60 ML) OLIVE OIL

½ CUP (25 G) PANKO BREAD CRUMBS

2 TABLESPOONS FINELY CHOPPED FRESH FLAT-LEAF PARSLEY

1 CUP (115 G) GRATED PARMESAN CHEESE

KOSHER SALT AND FRESHLY GROUND PEPPER

FOR THE GRANCH

1½ CUPS (375 G) PLAIN GREEK YOGURT

2 TABLESPOONS FRESH LEMON JUICE

¼ CUP (10 G) CHOPPED FRESH CHIVES

1 TABLESPOON FINELY CHOPPED FRESH DILL

1 TABLESPOON FINELY CHOPPED FRESH FLAT-LEAF PARSLEY

1½ TEASPOONS GRANULATED GARLIC

KOSHER SALT AND FRESHLY GROUND PEPPER

Place a rack in the upper third of the oven and preheat to 425°F (220°C).

In a large bowl, toss together the carrots and oil. In another bowl, stir together the panko, parsley, and cheese, and season with salt and pepper. Sprinkle the panko mixture over the carrots and toss gently. Transfer the carrots to a baking sheet and spread in a single layer. If any panko mixture is remaining in the bowl, sprinkle it over the carrots and press gently to adhere. Roast until the carrots are just tender and the panko is crisp, 10–15 minutes. Let cool slightly.

Meanwhile, make the granch: In a bowl, stir together the yogurt, lemon juice, chives, dill, parsley, and granulated garlic, and season with salt and pepper.

Serve the carrot fries warm with the granch for dipping.

PARMESAN STRAWS

To enhance the flavor of these crispy, crowd-pleasing snacks, add
1-2 tablespoons of chopped fresh herbs, such as rosemary or thyme,
to the cheese before sprinkling it onto the puff pastry.

ALL-PURPOSE FLOUR, FOR DUSTING

1 SHEET (14 OZ/440 G) FROZEN PUFF PASTRY, THAWED FOR 20 MINUTES

2 CUPS (250 G) GRATED PARMESAN CHEESE

FRESHLY GROUND PEPPER

Line 2 baking sheets with parchment paper.

On a very lightly floured work surface, roll out the puff pastry into a 10-by-16-inch
(25-by-40-cm) rectangle about ⅛ inch (3 mm) thick. Sprinkle with 1 cup (110 g) of
the cheese and season with pepper. Using the rolling pin, gently roll the pastry to
press the cheese into it, smoothing out any seams or wrinkles. Fold the pastry in half
crosswise and roll out again into a 10-by-16-inch (25-by-40-cm) rectangle. Sprinkle
with the remaining 1 cup (110 g) cheese and season with pepper, then repeat the
folding and rolling process. Using a sharp knife or a pastry cutter, cut the pastry
crosswise into long strips, each about 1 inch (2.5 cm) wide.

Transfer the strips to the prepared baking sheets, spacing them about 1 inch (2.5 cm)
apart. As you place each strip down, carefully twist the ends in opposite directions to
give the straws a spiraled look. If they start to untwist, gently press the ends into the
parchment to make them stick. Refrigerate for at least 10 minutes or up to 1 hour.

Preheat the oven to 375°F (190°C).

Bake the straws until deep golden brown, 15–20 minutes. Transfer the baking sheets
to wire racks. Let the straws stand on the baking sheets until they are cool and dry to
the touch, about 15 minutes. The straws are best served the day they are made.

TAMARI-MAPLE MIXED NUTS

Tamari, a Japanese form of soy sauce, has a richer flavor, darker color, and thicker texture than the common Chinese variety, making it an ideal ingredient in this salty, sweet, and spicy coating for mixed nuts.

1 CUP (115 G) RAW ALMONDS

½ CUP (60 G) RAW CASHEWS

½ CUP (60 G) RAW PISTACHIOS

3 TABLESPOONS TAMARI

3 TABLESPOONS PURE MAPLE SYRUP

2 TABLESPOONS SESAME SEEDS

¼ TEASPOON CAYENNE PEPPER

½ TEASPOON FLAKY SEA SALT

Preheat the oven to 350°F (180°C). Line a baking sheet with parchment paper or a silicone baking mat.

Spread the almonds, cashews, and pistachios in a single layer on the prepared baking sheet and toast for 5 minutes.

Meanwhile, in a large bowl, whisk together the tamari, maple syrup, sesame seeds, and cayenne.

Remove the nuts from the oven, add to the bowl with the tamari mixture, and toss to coat evenly. Spread the nuts in a single layer and sprinkle with the sea salt. Bake until the nuts are lightly browned and smell toasty, about 12 minutes. Transfer the parchment paper to a wire rack and let the nuts cool for 10 minutes. Using a spatula, transfer the nuts to a bowl, breaking apart any clumps.

Store in an airtight container at room temperature for up to 3 days.

Many brands of tamari are made without wheat, making it a good gluten-free substitute for traditional soy sauce.

DEVILS ON HORSEBACK

These sweet and salty warm appetizers are a take on the renowned British dish Angels on Horseback (oysters wrapped in bacon). You can also wrap the dates with bacon instead of prosciutto and swap in goat cheese for the blue cheese.

12 DATES
¼ LB (110 G) BLUE CHEESE
5 OZ (140 G) THINLY SLICED PROSCIUTTO, CUT INTO 12 LONG STRIPS

Preheat the oven to 400°F. Place 12 toothpicks in a small bowl filled with hot water and soak for 10 minutes, then drain. Line a baking sheet with parchment paper.

Using a paring knife, cut the dates in half lengthwise, removing the pits and being careful not to cut all the way through. Place a small amount of cheese in the center of each date, then press the date gently on each side to close the opening. Wrap a strip of prosciutto around each date and secure with a toothpick.

Place the dates on the prepared baking sheet. Bake until the prosciutto is crispy and the cheese is oozing out of the dates, about 10 minutes. Serve hot.

CRISPY CURRIED CHICKPEAS

Serve these fragrant, curry-coated nibbles with a refreshing citrus-based cocktail such as our Coconut Cream & Lime Margarita (page 64). These crunchy, sweet-and-spicy chickpeas are best enjoyed on the day they are made.

2 CANS (15 OZ /470 G EACH) CHICKPEAS, DRAINED, RINSED, AND PATTED DRY

2 TABLESPOONS CANOLA OIL

2 TABLESPOONS CURRY POWDER

1 TABLESPOON FIRMLY PACKED BROWN SUGAR

1 TEASPOON KOSHER SALT, PLUS SALT FOR SPRINKLING (OPTIONAL)

½ TEASPOON FRESHLY GROUND PEPPER

Preheat the oven to 400°F (205°C). Line a baking sheet with parchment paper.

In a large bowl, stir together the chickpeas, oil, curry powder, brown sugar, salt, and pepper until the chickpeas are evenly coated. Spread in a single layer on the prepared baking sheet. Roast until the chickpeas are crisp, golden, and fragrant, 35–40 minutes, stirring once halfway through. Sprinkle with more salt just before serving, if desired.

SYRUPS, MIXERS & MORE

SIMPLE SYRUP

1 cup (250 ml) water

1 cup (200 g) sugar

Infuser (see options below)

In a small saucepan over medium-high heat, bring the water to a simmer. Add the sugar and infuser of choice, if using, and stir until the sugar is dissolved. Remove from the heat and let cool. Strain the syrup through a fine-mesh sieve into a clean container, cover, and refrigerate for up to 2 weeks.

Makes about 1½ cups (375 ml)

INFUSER OPTIONS

Basil: 15 fresh basil leaves, roughly chopped

Gingerbread: 10 whole cloves, 2 cinnamon sticks 2-inch (5-cm) piece peeled fresh ginger, 1 teaspoon ground cinnamon, 1 teaspoon ground ginger

Hibiscus: ½ cup (15 g) dried hibiscus flowers

Lavender: 1 tablespoon dried lavender (strain cooled syrup through cheesecloth)

Lemongrass: 1 lemongrass stalk, thinly sliced

Rose: Substitute ¼ cup (60 ml) rose water for the same amount of plain water

Rosemary: 5 fresh rosemary sprigs, roughly chopped

Rosemary-Ginger: 2 tablespoons *each* chopped fresh rosemary and peeled fresh ginger

Sage: 10 fresh sage leaves, roughly chopped

Tarragon: 5 fresh tarragon sprigs

Thyme: 10 fresh thyme sprigs

Vanilla: 2 vanilla beans, split and seeds scraped

CINNAMON-APPLE SYRUP

¾ cup (180 ml) apple cider

¼ cup (45 ml) honey

½ teaspoon ground cinnamon

In a small saucepan over medium-high heat, combine the apple cider and honey and bring to a simmer. Add the cinnamon and stir until dissolved. Remove from the heat and let cool. Pour the syrup into a clean storage container. Use at once, or cover and refrigerate for up to 2 weeks.

Makes about 1 cup (250 ml)

STRAWBERRY-BASIL SYRUP

1 cup (150 g) whole strawberries, hulled

1 cup (200 g) sugar

1 tablespoon fresh lemon juice

¼ cup (7 g) fresh basil leaves

In a saucepan over medium-high heat, combine the strawberries, sugar, lemon juice, and basil and bring to a simmer. Reduce the heat to medium-low and continue to simmer, stirring frequently, until the berries have broken down and become juicy, about 20 minutes. Strain the syrup through a fine-mesh sieve into a clean container, cover, and refrigerate for up to 5 days.

Makes about 1 cup (240 ml)

VARIATION: BLACKBERRY-THYME SYRUP
Replace the strawberries with 1 cup (115 g) blackberries and the basil leaves with 2 fresh thyme sprigs.

AGAVE SYRUP

1 cup (250 ml) agave nectar

In a small saucepan over medium heat, bring 1 cup (250 ml) water to a simmer. Add the agave nectar and stir until the sugar is dissolved. Remove from the heat and let cool. Pour the syrup into a storage container. Use at once, or cover and refrigerate for up to 2 weeks.

Makes about 1 cup (250 ml)

CHERRY ICE CUBES

1 cup (250 ml) tart cherry juice
6 frozen or fresh cherries, pitted

In a large liquid measuring cup, stir together the cherry juice and 1 cup (250 ml) water. Pour into 6 large ice cube molds. Add 1 cherry to each mold and freeze overnight or for up to 3 months.

Makes 6 large ice cubes

BLACKBERRY COULIS

4 cups (450 g) fresh blackberries
2 tablespoons fresh lemon juice

In a blender, combine the blackberries and lemon juice and blend until smooth. Strain the blackberry coulis through a fine-mesh sieve into a container. Use at once, or cover and refrigerate for up to 2 days.

Makes ½ cup (125 ml)

SALTED CARAMEL

1 cup (200 g) sugar
6 tablespoons (80 g) unsalted butter, cut into 1-inch (2.5-cm) pieces, at room temperature
½ cup (125 ml) heavy cream
1½ teaspoons kosher salt

Put the sugar in a saucepan, set over medium-low heat, and heat, stirring occasionally, until the sugar is melted and golden brown, about 7 minutes. Add the butter, one piece at a time, and stir until melted. Slowly stir in in the cream; the mixture will begin to bubble. Cook, stirring occasionally, until the cream is incorporated and the caramel begins to thicken, about 10 minutes. Raise the heat to medium and cook, stirring occasionally, until the caramel is thickened and shiny, about 3 minutes. Add the salt and cook for 1 minute longer. Transfer the caramel to a heatproof container and let cool. Use at once, or cover and refrigerate for up 1 week.

Makes about 1 cup (250 ml)

CUCUMBER JUICE

1 cucumber, roughly chopped

In a blender, combine the cucumber and 1 tablespoon water and blend until smooth. Strain the cucumber juice through a fine-mesh sieve into a storage container. Use at once, or cover and refrigerate for up to 1 day.

Makes about ⅔ cup (160 ml)

INDEX

A

Agave Syrup, 93
Amaretto Affogato, 76
Apple & Honey Bee's Knees, 29
Apple-Spice Hot Toddy, 81

B

Bar snacks
  Brown Butter & Rosemary
    Popcorn, 82
  Carrot Fries with Granch, 86
  Citrus & Herb Marinated Olives, 83
  Crispy Curried Chickpeas, 91
  Devils on Horseback, 90
  Parmesan Straws, 87
  Tamari-Maple Mixed Nuts, 88
Bar essentials, 13
Bar tools, 8
Basil
  Basil Julep, 52
  Basil Simple Syrup, 92
  Strawberry-Basil Mimosa, 70
  Strawberry-Basil Syrup, 92
Bitters, about, 13
Blackberry Coulis, 93
Blackberry Lemonade Whiskey
  Sour, 55
Blackberry-Thyme Bellini, 75
Blackberry-Thyme Syrup, 92
Bourbon
  Apple-Spice Hot Toddy, 81
  Basil Julep, 52
  Vanilla-Citrus Old-Fashioned, 55

C

Carrot Fries with Granch, 86
Cherry Ice Cubes, 93
Chickpeas, Crispy Curried, 91
Cinnamon-Apple Syrup, 92
Classic Cocktails, 12–13
Coconut Cream & Lime Margarita, 64
Coffee
  Amaretto Affogato, 76
  Salted Caramel Irish Coffee, 81
Cranberry-Tequila Punch, 58

Cucumbers
  Cucumber Juice, 93
  Tequila & Ancho Reyes with
    Cucumber, 62

D

Devils on Horseback, 90

E

Edible flowers, 28
Elderflower-Rose Collins, 35

F

French 75 with Lavender & Lemon, 30

G

Garnishing ideas, 42–43
Gin
  Apple & Honey Bee's Knees, 29
  Elderflower-Rose Collins, 35
  French 75 with Lavender
    & Lemon, 30
  Grapefruit & Sage Gimlet, 33
  Lemongrass Last Word, 30
  Lime & Thyme Gin Fizz, 34
  Pegu Cocktail, 35
  Ramos Gin Fizz, 33
  Spanish Gin & Tonic, 29
  Sparkling Corpse Reviver, 34
  Tarragon Negroni, 36
Ginger
  Gingerbread Dark & Stormy, 45
  Gingerbread Simple Syrup, 92
  Rosemary-Ginger Mojito, 46
  Rosemary-Ginger Simple Syrup, 92
Ginger beer
  Gingerbread Dark & Stormy, 45
  Meyer Lemon–Rosemary Moscow
    Mule, 24
Glassware, 9
Grapefruit
  Grapefruit & Sage Gimlet, 33
  Mint Hemingway Daiquiri, 44
  St-Germain Greyhound, 24
  Tarragon Paloma, 63

H

Hibiscus Simple Syrup, 13
Hibiscus & Tart Cherry Manhattan, 51

I

Ice Cubes, Cherry, 93
Ice cubes and crushed ice, 18–19
Ice Pops, Piña Colada, 76

J

Juices, fresh, 13

L

Lavender
  French 75 with Lavender
    & Lemon, 30
  Lavender Simple Syrup, 92
Lemon
  Blackberry Lemonade Whiskey
    Sour, 55
  French 75 with Lavender
    & Lemon, 30
  Hard Watermelon Lemonade, 78
  Meyer Lemon–Rosemary Moscow
    Mule, 24
  Sparkling Lemon & Raspberry
    Float, 70
Lemongrass Last Word, 30
Lemongrass Simple Syrup, 92
Lillet
  Sparkling Corpse Reviver, 34
  Strawberry-Lillet Vodka Soda, 16
  Tarragon Negroni, 36
Lime
  Basil Julep, 52
  Coconut Cream & Lime
    Margarita, 64
  Lemongrass Last Word, 30
  Lime & Thyme Gin Fizz, 34
  Lychee & Lime Sake Cocktail, 75
  Mint Hemingway Daiquiri, 44
  Rosemary-Ginger Mojito, 46
  Tequila & Ancho Reyes with
    Cucumber, 62

Liqueurs, about, 13
Lychee & Lime Sake Cocktail, 75

M

Mango Mai Tai, 41
Mint
  Hard Watermelon Lemonade, 78
  Mint Hemingway Daiquiri, 44
  Rosemary-Ginger Mojito, 46
Mixers, 92–93

N

Nuts, Tamari-Maple Mixed, 88

O

Olives, Citrus & Herb Marinated, 83
Oranges
  Blood Orange Cosmopolitan, 21
  Citrus & Herb Marinated Olives, 83
  Pegu Cocktail, 35
  Pomegranate Martini, 23
  Rosé Sangria with Citrus
    & Raspberries, 69
  Tequila Sunrise with Pineapple
    & Jalapeño, 61
  Vanilla-Citrus Old-Fashioned, 55

P

Parmesan Straws, 87
Peach-Raspberry Frozen Daiquiri, 79
Pegu Cocktail, 35
Peppermint White Russian, 20
Piña Colada Ice Pops, 76
Pineapple
  Mango Mai Tai, 41
  Piña Colada Ice Pops, 76
  Tequila Sunrise with Pineapple
    & Jalapeño, 61
Pomegranate Martini, 23
Popcorn, Brown Butter & Rosemary, 82

R

Ramos Gin Fizz, 33
Raspberries
  Raspberry-Peach Frozen Daiquiri, 79
  Rosé Sangria with Citrus &
    Raspberries, 69
  Sparkling Lemon & Raspberry
    Float, 70

Rosemary
  Brown Butter & Rosemary
    Popcorn, 82
  Citrus & Herb Marinated Olives, 83
  Cranberry-Tequila Punch, 58
  Meyer Lemon–Rosemary Moscow
    Mule, 24
  Rosemary-Ginger Mojito, 46
  Rosemary-Ginger Simple Syrup, 92
  Rosemary Simple Syrup, 92
Rosé Sangria with Citrus
  & Raspberries, 69
Rose water
  Elderflower-Rose Collins, 35
  Rose Simple Syrup, 92
Rum
  Gingerbread Dark & Stormy, 45
  Mango Mai Tai, 41
  Mint Hemingway Daiquiri, 44
  Piña Colada Ice Pops, 76
  Raspberry-Peach Frozen Daiquiri, 79
  Rosemary-Ginger Mojito, 46

S

Sage
  Grapefruit & Sage Gimlet, 33
  Sage Simple Syrup, 92
Sake Cocktail, Lychee & Lime, 75
Salted Caramel, 93
Salted Caramel Irish Coffee, 81
Simple Syrup, 92
Spanish Gin & Tonic, 29
St-Germain
  Elderflower-Rose Collins, 35
  St-Germain Greyhound, 24
Strawberry-Basil Mimosa, 70
Strawberry-Basil Syrup, 92
Strawberry-Lillet Vodka Soda, 16
Syrups
  Agave Syrup, 93
  Blackberry-Thyme Syrup, 92
  Cinnamon-Apple Syrup, 92
  Gingerbread Simple Syrup, 92
  infusing with flavors, 92
  Simple Syrup, 92
  Strawberry-Basil Syrup, 92

T

Tamari-Maple Mixed Nuts, 88
Tarragon Negroni, 36

Tarragon Paloma, 63
Tarragon Simple Syrup, 92
Tequila
  Coconut Cream & Lime
    Margarita, 64
  Cranberry-Tequila Punch, 58
  Tarragon Paloma, 63
  Tequila & Ancho Reyes with
    Cucumber, 62
  Tequila Sunrise with Pineapple
    & Jalapeño, 61
Thyme
  Blackberry-Thyme Bellini, 75
  Blackberry-Thyme Syrup, 92
  Citrus & Herb Marinated Olives, 83
  Lime & Thyme Gin Fizz, 34
  Thyme Simple Syrup, 92

V

Vanilla-Citrus Old-Fashioned, 55
Vanilla Simple Syrup, 92
Vermouth
  about, 13
  Hibiscus & Tart Cherry Manhattan, 51
Vodka
  Blood Orange Cosmopolitan, 21
  Hard Watermelon Lemonade, 78
  Meyer Lemon–Rosemary Moscow
    Mule, 24
  Peppermint White Russian, 20
  Pomegranate Martini, 23
  St-Germain Greyhound, 24
  Strawberry-Lillet Vodka Soda, 16

W

Watermelon Lemonade, Hard, 78
Whiskey
  Blackberry Lemonade Whiskey Sour, 55
  Hibiscus & Tart Cherry Manhattan, 51
  Smoky Maple Sazerac, 51
Wine and sparkling wine
  Blackberry-Thyme Bellini, 75
  Cranberry-Tequila Punch, 58
  French 75 with Lavender & Lemon, 30
  Rosé Sangria with Citrus
    & Raspberries, 69
  Sparkling Lemon & Raspberry Float, 70
  Strawberry-Basil Mimosa, 70

COCKTAILS

Conceived and produced by Weldon Owen, Inc.
In collaboration with Williams Sonoma, Inc.
3250 Van Ness Avenue, San Francisco, CA 94109

A WELDON OWEN PRODUCTION

1150 Brickyard Cove Road
Richmond, CA 94801
www.weldonowen.com

Copyright © 2017 Weldon Owen, Inc.
and Williams Sonoma, Inc.
All rights reserved, including the right of reproduction
in whole or in part in any form.

Printed and bound in China

10 9 8 7 6 5 4

Library of Congress Cataloging-in-Publication
data is available.

ISBN: 978-1-68188-268-0

WELDON OWEN, INC.

President & Publisher Roger Shaw
SVP, Sales & Marketing Amy Kaneko
Finance & Operations Director Thomas Morgan

Associate Publisher Amy Marr
Senior Editor Lisa Atwood

Creative Director Kelly Booth
Art Director Marisa Kwek
Production Designer Howie Severson

Associate Production Director Michelle Duggan
Imaging Manager Don Hill

Photographer John Kernick
Food Stylist Hadas Smirnoff
Prop Stylist Alistair Turnbull

ACKNOWLEDGMENTS

Weldon Owen wishes to thank the following people for their generous support in producing
this book: Rizwan A. Alvi, Kris Balloun, Julian Bolton, Cocktail Kingdom, Josephine Hsu,
Alexis Mersel, Carolyn Miller, Elizabeth Parson, Sharon Silva, Annelizabeth Wells, and Tamara White.